Hobo & Tramp Art Carving

Hobo & Tramp Art Carving

An Authentic American Folk Tradition

Adolph Vandertie
with Patrick Spielman

Sterling Publishing Co., Inc. New York
A Sterling/Chapelle Book

For Chapelle Limited

Owner: Jo Packham

Staff: Trice Boerens, Malissa Boatwright,
Rebecca Christensen, Holly Fuller,
Cherie Hanson, Holly Hollingsworth,
Susan Jorgensen, Susan Laws,
Amanda McPeck, Barbara Milburn,
Leslie Ridenour, Cindy Stoeckl,
and Nancy Whitley

Photography: Ryne Hazen

A special thanks is extended to Ray Sauvey and
Terry C. Misfeldt of the National Railroad Museum located
in Green Bay, WI, for their trust and hospitality in allowing
us to photograph in their lovely facility.

Poems by Charles Elmer Fox used by permission of University of Iowa Press.

Photos on pages 2, 13, and 17 are used courtesy of the Library of Congress.

Library of Congress Cataloging-in-Publication Data

Vandertie, Adolph, 1911-
   Hobo & tramp art carving : an authentic American folk tradition /
  Adolph Vandertie with Patrick Spielman.
      p.   cm.
   Includes index.
   ISBN 0-8069-3185-X
   1. Wood-carving--United States--Patterns. 2. Tramp art. 3. Folk
art--United States. I. Spielman, Patrick E. II. Title.
TT199.7.V36 1995
731.4'62--dc20
                                          95-16331
                                          CIP

10 9 8 7 6 5 4 3 2 1

A Sterling/Chapelle Book

Published by Sterling Publishing Company, Inc.
387 Park Avenue South, New York, N.Y. 10016
© 1995 by Chapelle Ltd.
Distributed in Canada by Sterling Publishing
℅ Canadian Manda Group, One Atlantic Avenue, Suite 105
Toronto, Ontario, Canada M6K 3E7
Distributed in Great Britain and Europe by Cassell PLC
Wellington House, 125 Strand, London WC2R 0BB, England
Distributed in Australia by Capricorn Link (Australia) Pty Ltd.
P.O. Box 6651, Baulkham Hills, Business Center, NSW 2153, Australia
Printed and bound in Hong Kong
All Rights Reserved

Sterling ISBN 0-8069-3185-X

*T*o my best friend, partner and wife, Adeline, who, for more than 60 years, has endured my spending much time in pursuit of hobo art and tramp art and has helped in every aspect of my activities — including sweeping up numerous piles of wood chips.

— Adolph Vandertie

Contents

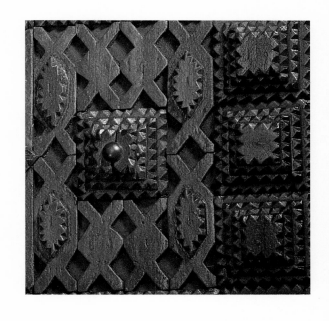

From the Author

I was born about four miles south of Lena, Wisconsin in a little log cabin. The cabin was built by my father's and mother's brothers on 40 acres of land that was given to my father as part of my mother's wedding dowry. I was born on May 25, 1911, one of a set of twins. My parents had two sets of twins and a total of ten children. Seven of us were born in that cabin. There was a total of nine people that lived in that little building that was only 16 x 20 feet. We moved from Lena to Green Bay in 1919 or 1920.

The obsession I have with whittling and the collecting of hobo and tramp art began when, as a young boy, I made frequent trips to the hobo jungles in Green Bay. There, I listened, wide-eyed, to the stories told by the hoboes. These stories, that I so loved to hear, told to me by these colorful wanderers of faraway places they had been and the many adventures they had experienced were not all necessarily true, but they were magic to an impressionable young boy. It was in these hobo jungles that I ate my first Mulligan stew and learned the art and trademark of the whittler: the ball-in-the-cage and the chain.

As is inevitable to all of us, there comes a time when a young boy's dreams and fantasies must give way to the harsh realities of earning a living and raising a family.

So it was that I postponed learning more of the life and the art of the hobo. The postponement lasted for what seemed to me a very long time; as a matter of fact, it continued until I was faced with the decision to quit smoking 40 some odd years ago (I am now 84).

I needed something to keep my hands and mind occupied. Something to keep me from incessantly clawing at my pocket for a cigarette that was not there. So with some perseverance and determination, I soon developed yet another habit. The habit of reaching for my pocketknife and a piece of wood, thereby developing a second addiction—that of whittling!

Over the past 43 years I have collected and whittled an estimated 4,000 pieces of whittler's art. In fact, I became so fascinated with the ball-in-the-cage and the chain that I have included one or both in almost all of the pieces I have whittled myself. In addition to the hundreds of pieces with balls-in-the-cage, my collection includes more than 350 chains of various designs and lengths. These chains range from 8 inches to one that is 217 feet long, weighs less than 2 pounds, and has 2,821 links. This unusual record-breaking chain appeared in *Ripely's Believe It Or Not* several years ago.

My rediscovered preoccupation with whittling eventually led me to a small town in north central Iowa called Britt, the hobo capital of the United States. Yearly, since 1903, the National Hobo Convention is held there and the King and Queen of the hoboes are elected. This royalty is selected from such notable names as Sparky Smith, Fry Pan Jack, Mountain Dew, Iowa Blackie, Frisco Jack, Mr. Nobody, The Pennsylvania Kid, The Hard Rock Kid, John Mislen, Virginia Slim, Boxcar Johnnie, Portland Grey, Hand Bag Annie, Toledo Ruth and one neophyte from Wisconsin who earned the title of the Official Hobo Whittler. The present King is Steam Train Maury Graham of Toledo, Ohio, and the Queen is Long Looker MicDensild of Iowa.

My purpose for going to Britt was to research the art, the history, and the philosophy of these wandering nomads of the rails. I came away with a clearer understanding of these people called hobos and the people called tramps, and the differences in their lives and in their art.

There are only an estimated dozen or so "real" rail-riding hoboes left in the United States, and because most of them are very old, I believe this to be the last generation. For this reason, I am most anxious to preserve not only their memories, but also the few remaining artifacts of their art and their culture for future generations to enjoy.

My plans for preserving these magnificent pieces of original American folk art involve negotiations with several museums and related organizations that will provide a permanent repository for my entire collection. For the present, however, my home is a live-in museum where my collection is always on display.

Adolph Vandertie

History of Hobo Art

For almost eighty years in America's history, the time between the Civil War and the Second World War, teenage boys dreamed of becoming hoboes. To them, the excitement of hopping a moving freight train, riding the rods beneath the passenger car, or outsmarting the railroad officials was equaled by no other dream. To these young men, hoboing was the ultimate test of manhood. It took courage, strength, skill, imagination, daring, and endurance to live on the road. And even though the reality of hobo life proved to be lonely, brutal, and often tragic, some considered their days riding the rails to be the best times of their lives.

The American hobo was probably one of the most maligned, misunderstood, and exploited members of American society. To better understand the true nature of the hobo, one needs only interpret one origin of the word hobo, which is derived from the English use of the term "hoe boys." This term was used to refer to the people who worked and hoed the gardens and estates of the very wealthy. In other words, the hobo was the original migrant worker. In America, these wandering workers were fairly common by the eighteenth century. Because there were no railroads, most of these men would suddenly appear in villages fairly near their home seeking work.

After the Civil War, the Industrial Revolution exploded across America and, with this rapid industrial growth and the development of the rail road, came the birth and the growth of the world of the American hobo. The true hobo was basically a laboring man of many trades and many talents who wandered the country in search of work.

He laid and repaired railroad track, harvested wheat, cut down trees, mined for gold, herded cattle, built bridges and then moved on. When the Depression hit this country and the times swung from prosperous to destitute, these hard times produced the hobo that we often think of today. By the end of the nineteenth century, it is estimated that more than a million men were on the road, riding the rails, looking for work. It was his constant wandering that made the hobo such a distinct and mythical character.

Without trains, there would not have been hoboes. Traveling was at the heart of hobo life, and the trains provided the means for that travel. A hobo did not pay a fare to ride the rails like the traditional passenger, instead he "flipped" freight trains—or jumped on board without paying. While a few specialized in passenger trains, which were the most difficult and dangerous to ride, most hoboes preferred to jump freight trains. To escape the detection of the men hired by the railroads—the railroad bulls—the hobo would hide in the coal of the coal cars or among cattle in the cattle cars. Riding a train became an art form and a matter survival for the hobo. A hobo's life depended upon knowing how to correctly board a train and ride on it, in it, or under it.

The hoboes lived by their own code of law and honor, authored their own stories, composed their own songs, developed their own customs, and wrote their own language. They were members of a new society who discarded their real names and identities and replaced them with names of the road, such as Feather River John "Mcloughey," Fry Pan Jack, Box Car Willie and Frisco Jack.

Most hoboes were intelligent, worldly, and amazingly eloquent. Steam Train Maury has often been quoted as saying "Do not ever confuse a hobo with a bum! A bum is shiftless and worthless. A hobo is a man of the world, who travels to see and observe and then shares those views with others." Steam Train has also been quoted in stories that testify to the authenticity of Ernest Hemingway, Jack London, and Art Linkletter spending a number of years as hoboes, gathering experiences and backgrounds before they began their writing and acting careers.

There is very little written about the leisure time of the hobo, but it is known that he was a stick whittler. He came about it naturally because he carried a jackknife, his most valuable tool, in his pocket; and wood was always available. So, with little else to do with his time, it was natural that he should learn to whittle.

The results of this whittling make up one of the original forms of American folk art, or hobo art. Hobo art consists mostly of objects that contain the ball-in-the-cage or the chain. They were objects of a more whimsical nature that were less utilitarian than the tramp art that is discussed in Tramp Art History.

To produce any of these fascinating pieces, the whittler needed only a piece of wood, his pocketknife and a sharpening stone. He, like the tramp, would then use his pieces to give as a gift to a friend, barter for food, or exchange for money.

Knives & Sharpening

1. The three-bladed knife offers a choice of sizes for different kinds of cuts or special jobs. Note how small some of the blades have become through repeated sharpenings. Smaller and thinner blades allow for producing smaller and more detailed work.

The Barlow knife became the most popular knife design in American history. Designed by a man named Barlow, this two-bladed jackknife, referred to as the working man's knife, is now manufactured by many companies. It has one large blade and one smaller "pen" blade for finer work.

2. Use a fine sharpening stone, unless the knife is very dull or nicked, in which case use the coarse stone (or coarse side). Lay the blade flat on the stone and at an angle to the edge of the stone as shown. Push the knife forward against the edge.

3. At the end of the push stroke, flip the blade entirely over and draw it toward you in a similar fashion as shown.

4. Stroping (also called honing): Hold the leather strop of the top of the sharpening stone so that you have some knuckle room above the bench or table surface. The knife is held similar to the sharpening position, except the edge of the knife is reversed and trailing the blade. This is necessary so you don't cut into the leather. *Note:* Work both surfaces of the blade equally. Once sharp, you need only to strop, or hone, it frequently during the course of your carving.

1. Left to right demonstrates the various steps of carving in the development of a combination ball-in-the-cage and chain.

2. Notching decorative cross-grain grooves with the pocketknife.

3. Preliminary stages in the carving of an unusual eight-sided triangular ball-in-cage project. Here the knife is cutting with the grain to establish the inside outline of the triangular-shaped cage.

Woods

The best woods to use for whittling are cedar, soft white or sugar pine, and basswood. They should be smooth and straight-grained. After you have worked with wood for a while, you will develop your own preferences and may even eventually acquire a preference for the harder woods. The wood must be soft enough so that it won't crack yet strong enough to hold once you have cut away a major portion of it.

Walking sticks made from chestnut or willow branches with designs carved in the bark such as these, are ideal practice projects for the would-be hobo art whittler. Simply knife-cut through the bark and peel it away. Notice the simple ring patterns and elementary designs.

Sliding Multiple Joint

DIRECTIONS

After completing the ball-in-the-cage on page 26, you may want to try this technique. For this project, use a square 5" length of soft wood.

1. Carve off the corners, making the wood eight-sided as in Diagram 1. Make sure all sides are equal in width.

2. Draw the design on the wood; see Diagram 2. Remove all the (A) sections. You will have very little room to work between the eight bars.

3. Carve the individual bars. Your cage should look like Diagram 3. For a more intricate shape, leave a ball inside as in Diagram 4.

Diagram 2

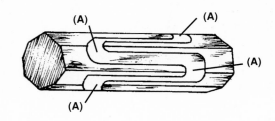

Diagram 1

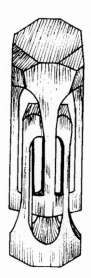

Diagram 3

Diagram 4

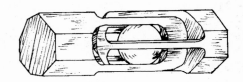

Ball-in-the-Cage

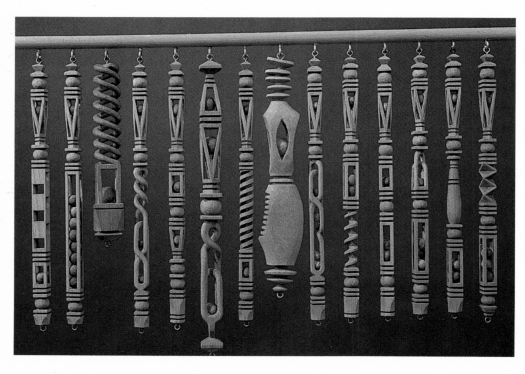

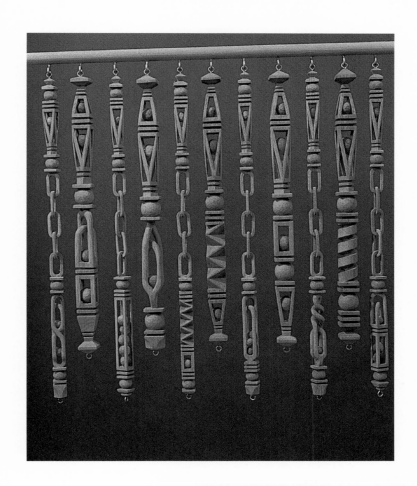

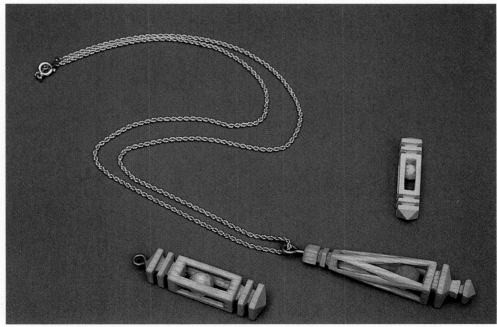

Ball-in-the-Cage

DIRECTIONS

You may use any length and diameter of wood you desire. For our example, we are using a block which is ¾" square and 3" long.

1. Starting ½" from each end, mark the design with pencil on all four sides as in Diagram 1. Cut the shaded portions clear through so that your block looks like Diagram 2.

2. You will now be working with section (A) Diagram 2, an enlargement of which is shown in Diagram 3. Cut as indicated by the dotted lines, freeing the central portion and leaving a bar along each corner connecting the two ends. Work carefully between the bars and round off the ends and sides of the center block to form a ball; see Diagram 4.

Variations: Try making the cage longer and place two balls inside or make your side bars in a spiral shape.

Diagram 1

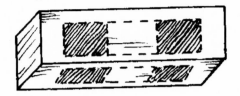

Diagram 2

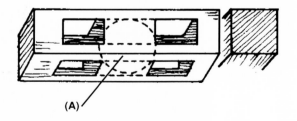

(A)

Diagram 3

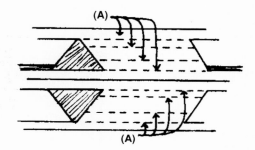

Diagram 4

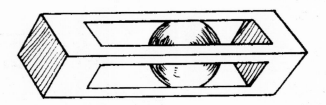

The Chain

The Chain

DIRECTIONS

For the chain, you will need a ⅝" square, straight-grain stick, any length you wish. For the beginner, a 6"-8" length would work best.

1. Following the dotted lines in Diagram 1, cut away the four wooden strips from the corners, leaving the stick in a cross shape. (Cutting the lines in Diagram 2 in a diamond shape will give you wider links.)

2. Mark off the first link on the prepared stick as in Diagram 3. (Links that are 1½ times the width of the stick are a good proportion.) Mark only the two opposite sides for the first link. Cut a small V-shaped groove along your mark (A to B); see Diagram 4. Repeat on the opposite side.

3. At the halfway mark of the first link on the alternate sides (C), cut V-shaped grooves as in Step 2. Repeat with the other side; see Diagram 5 (D). Cut away the shaded portion (E). Your stick should now look like Diagram 6.

4. Mark your first link along the dotted line on both sides as shown in Diagram 7. Cut away the shaded portion on both sides and your stick will look like Diagram 8. Repeat with second link, allowing your link to hang loose as in Diagram 9. Continue making as many links as you wish, being careful not to crush the links you have made.

5. Trim the corners and round off the links; see Diagram 10.

Diagram 1

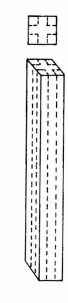

Diagram 2

(A)   (B)

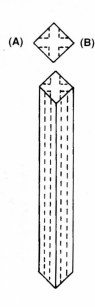

Diagram 3

Diagram 4

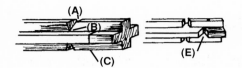

Diagram 5

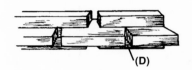

Diagram 6

Diagram 7

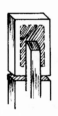

Diagram 8

Diagram 9

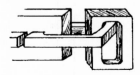

Diagram 10

Candlesticks

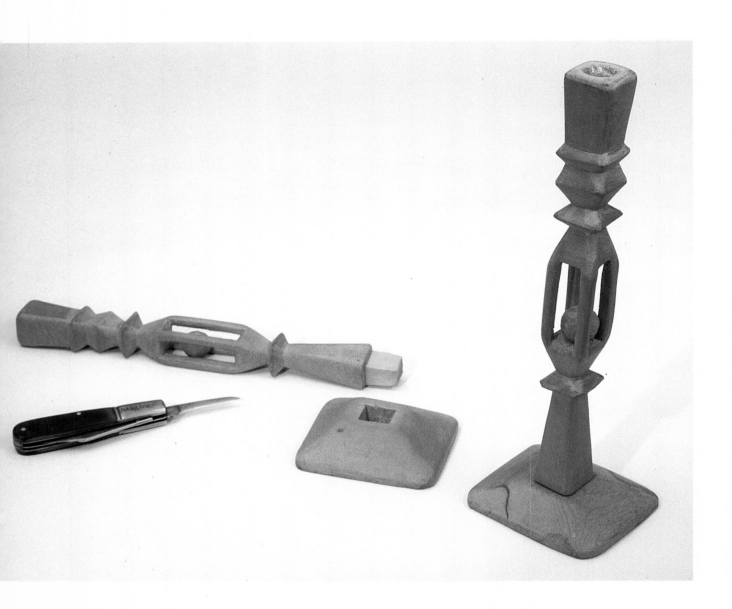

Candlestick, Full Size

Candlestick Base, Top View

Candlestick Base, Side View

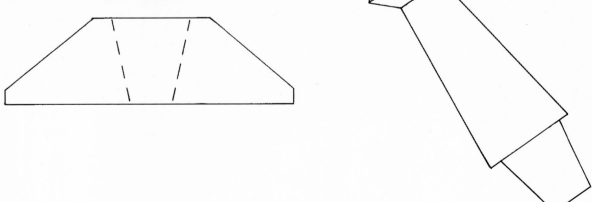

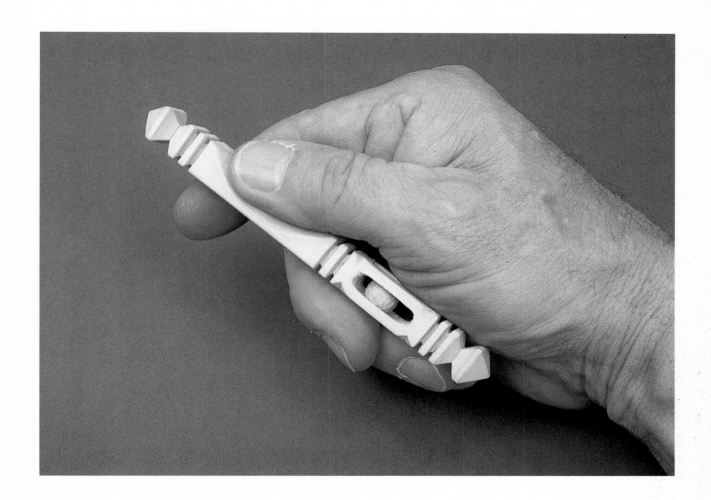

Fidget Stick

A fidget stick may prove to be a powerful remedy to the treatment of stress. Simply rub your thumb on the concave surface to calm the nerves; see page 37 for pattern.

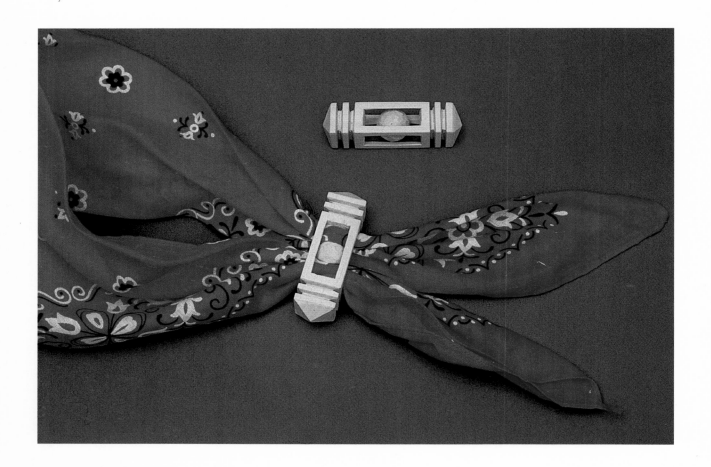

Neckerchief Slide

*T*he neckerchief slide is used to secure the red neckerchief, which is the symbol of the true rail-riding hobo; see opposite page for pattern. The ball-in-the-cage is the universal trademark of the whittler. Sooner or later, virtually every whittler will attempt carving a ball-in-the-cage because of the challenge it presents.

Fidget Stick, Full Size

Neckerchief Slide, Full Size

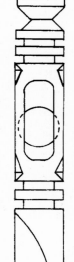

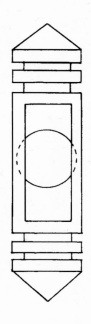

Gallery

In Memory Of Them All

Boxcars rattling in the rain,
The age-old song of a speeding train.
It takes me back to the long ago.
To Mulligan Shorty and Bug-eyed Joe.

I've sat with them by many fires,
When the days came to an end,
And heard a steam train whistle moan
As she came around the bend.

Off on some distant mountain grade
In the wee hours of the night,
The cracking exhaust of a steamer at work
And her piercing yellow light.

As the embers of the fire glow faintly
And the long hours of night pass on,
I think of old friends and the steamers I loved,
For all are now dead and gone.

— Charles Elmer Fox

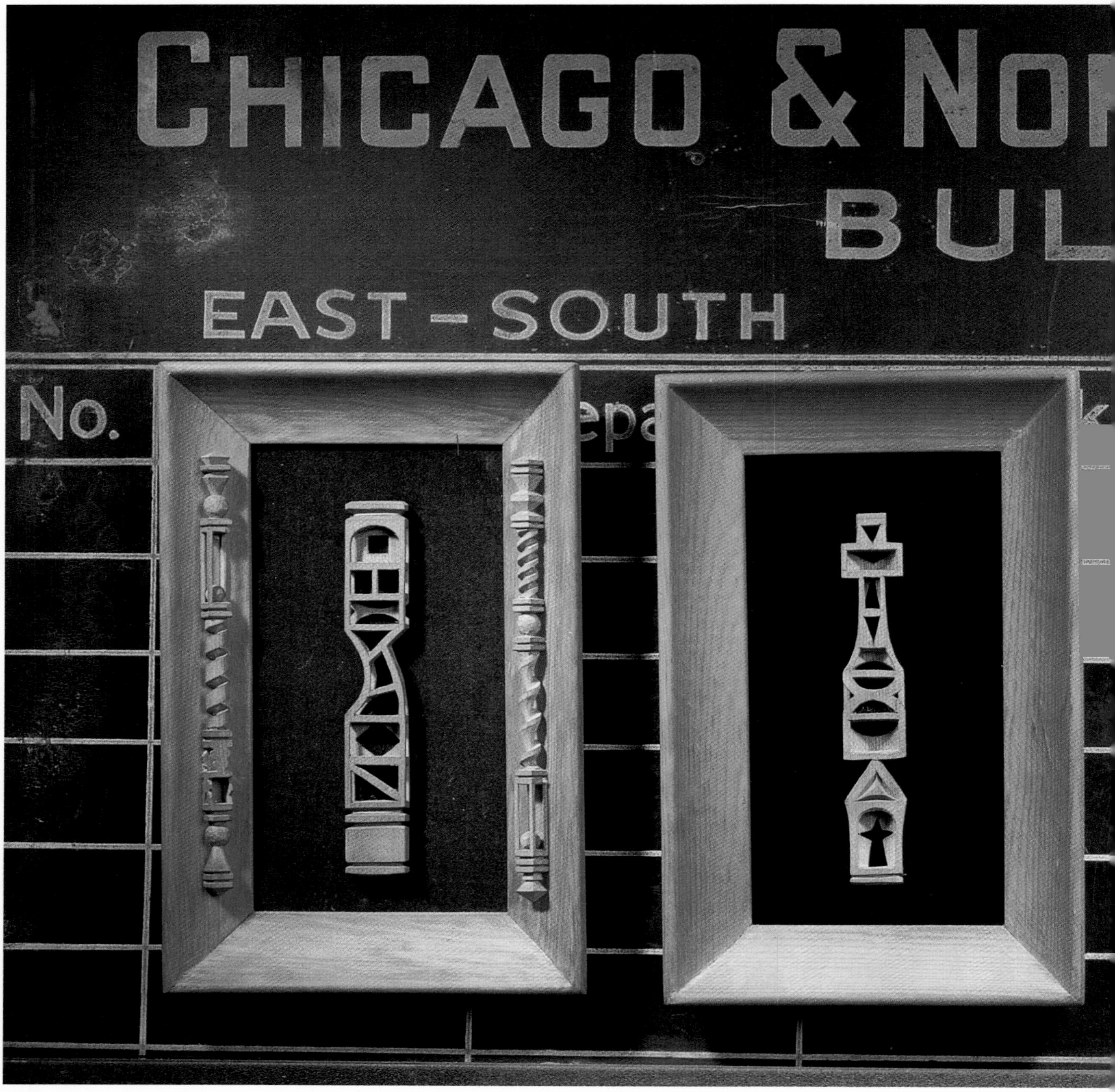
CHICAGO & NOR
BUL
EAST - SOUTH
No.

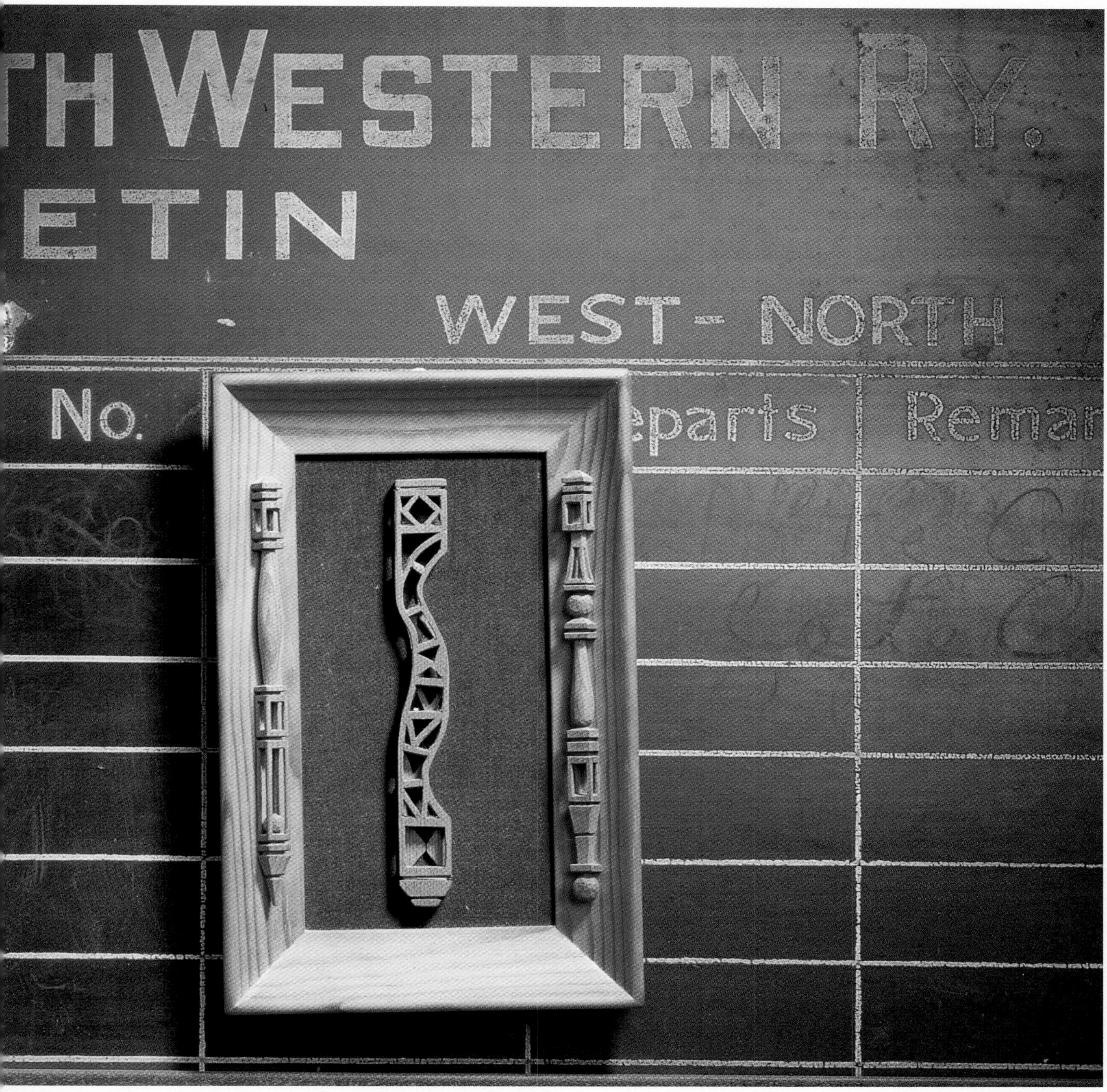
THWESTERN RY.
ETIN
WEST-NORTH
No.
eparts
Remar

Hobo Life

When springtime comes with balmy days,
And green things start to growing,
I'll get my pack and bedroll ready,
For soon I must be going.

I've spent the winter in a little shack
With a hobo pal of mine,
Saw the snow piled high, heard the cold wind blow
Through the limbs of a nearby pine.

Often at night when I'm tucked in bed
I'm awakened by an approaching train,
see the golden beam of her piercing light,
Hear the whistle's sweet refrain.

Spring brings joy to a hobo's heart,
No nicer time could be,
To ride the rails on the cinder trails,
My campfire pal and me.

— **Charles Elmer Fox**

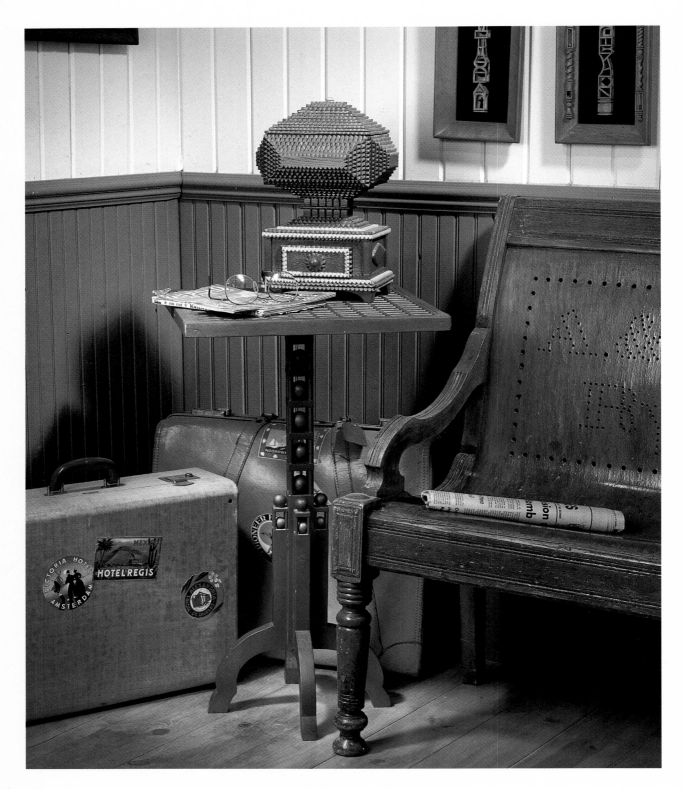

48 Hobo Art

Climbing Sherman Hill

I hear an echo from the past
Though the night is very still,
A compound Malley on a manifest
Pulling up Sherman Hill.

This hill is the trademark of old Cheyenne
As every bo doth know,
A beautiful sight at sunrise
In the morning's golden glow.

In the distance I see a little fire
Along the U.P. main,
Some hobo's camp by the water tower
Where he'll catch a westbound train.

Then I hear that lonesome whistle
As that Malley tops the hill
And heads on west to the sawtooth's
In the early morning chill.

— **Charles Elmer Fox**

The Last Hobo

I sit by the little campfire alone
Beside the railroad track.
My pals have caught that westbound freight
and they won't be coming back.

We never thought when we were young
That the day must surely come
When we'd ride our final westbound freight
To the land beyond the sun.

So thought this ancient vagabond
I'm the last of a kind to be.
I've worried about this these many years:
O why did the Lord pick me?

— Charles Elmer Fox

History of Tramp Art

Tramp Art is also a wanderer's art form: so again, there are no written records of the carvers' work. The stories of this art form became the facts; the misconceptions became the truths. There were no rules for constructing the pieces; materials were whatever the carver had available; decorations were whatever he could produce or find. Within the context of his own imagination, experience, and abilities, the carver assimilated what he saw with what he had to work with. He then translated and created what he saw into works of art by using his pocketknife and the ever-present cigar box.

Like the hobo, the tramp was a wanderer, but unlike the hobo, he was not a worker. Most tramps lived by their wits, some by petty thievery and begging, some by robbery and murder. The hobo feared the tramp and was contemptuous of him as a loafer, while the tramp despised the hobo as a sucker for working.

The distinction between tramps and hoboes, however, was not always discernable. Many men, and women, lived in both worlds, hoboing to make a "stake," then living without working until the stake ran out. Some hoboes became tramps, especially when there was no work to be found, and some tramps became hoboes. But even though tramps and hoboes often lived in different worlds, as far as work and philosophy were concerned, they were forced to share the same space. Hoboes and tramps together flipped the same trains, ate and slept in the same jungles, and were locked up together in the same jail cells.

The tramp world, however, had its own society separate with its own rules and its own hierarchy. At the top of the list was the "profesh," or professional tramp. He was

distinguishable because of his good clothes, his habits of neatness, and that he often slept on newspapers.

The typical tramp, as we think of him, was a "fakir." He was part conman and part repairman or apprentice of a trade, such as a tinsmith, carpenter, blacksmith, etc. Many fakirs were very skilled but preferred to wander from town to town, searching for work when they felt like it.

The common meeting ground of both hoboes and tramps was the "jungle". The jungle was a campsite, usually located outside of town near the railroad tracks. The jungle was a place where everyone was welcomed as long as they obeyed the rules. In the jungle, there was food, a place to sleep, and companionship. Both hoboes and tramps lived in a state of constant hunger, and rarely did either ever get enough food. The main meal, which was usually the main event of the day, was served in the evening, and was usually a large stew called "Mulligan Stew." Unless one was hurt or ill, to share in the meal one had to contribute. Those who did not bring food had to work as chefs or gather firewood, and everyone was required to clean up after himself.

Many tramps and hoboes were self-educated and widely read in economics and political philosophy. After dinner, the men would often sit around the fire and share not only their political views and discuss social isues, but they would also tell stories about the adventures they had lived, the fast trains they had ridden, and the jails they had been in. They spent a great deal of time sharing their knowledge of daily survival: which policemen and judges to avoid, which towns were friendly and which were hostile. Because hoboes and tramps were constantly on the road and had no access to telephones, telegraphs, or the mail, they developed a complex system of communication. There was a system of signs used to let hoboes and tramps know whatever a "friend" felt was important for another friend to know. There were signs to let newcomers know where they might find a friendly or hostile reception, directions to a welcoming place, or warnings for hostile dogs, police, or thieves.

Around these campfires they would also sing songs, recite poetry, and create their own individual works of art: the hoboes would whittle while the tramps would carve.

This relatively little known form of folk art, called "tramp art," was produced by these anonymous skilled artisans in the hobo jungles of the U.S. but was introduced in the early 1860s by the German and Scandinavian Wanderbuersons, or wandering apprentices. These men—the trampers—popularized chip carving as they traveled the U.S. countryside in search of jobs or in the pursuit of the vagabond life.

Chip carving had been used as a method of decorating wooden objects in Europe almost since the beginning of time. By using any sharp-edged tool, but most often a pocketknife, small chips of wood were removed from a larger piece to form geometric patterns. A simple V could be cut on the edge of a piece of wood, or an elaborate gouge covering a large surface could be used for more elaborate decoration. In the hobo jungles, it became commonplace for the trampers to combine chip carving and whittling when using their pocketknife on cigar boxes.

The availability of cigar-box wood was a major factor in the production of tramp art. In the 1850s, the wooden cigar box came into use both in the United States and Europe. Since it was difficult to ship cigars cheaply and easily for packing into boxes, wherever cigars were made, cigar boxes were made nearby.

At the turn of the twentieth century, cigar smoking was at its height because cigars were considered symbols of masculinity and affluence. Success bred competition, and competition meant advertising. As a result, cigars were magnificently boxed. Revenue laws did not permit the boxes to be used a second time for cigars, so enterprising souls found new uses for the boxes. Since the boxes were plentiful and easily carved, ornamenting them by chip carving became popular.

This technique of chip carving consisted of notching and layering, with each succeeding layer being a little smaller than the preceding one, to create a pyramidal design. One cigar box or many cigar boxes could be used for the frame of the piece as well as performing the decorative function. Either way, the carver had to have a great deal of time and patience to create his finished product. He had to notch-carve each individual piece of wood many times. Then he had to layer the individual notch-carved pieces of wood into some kind of recognizable object. And then he had to decide if he wanted to add further decorations to the piece. One of the most fascinating aspects of tramp art is the evident desire of the carver to produce detailed and often very skilled work with only make-do and simple tools. This layering of piece upon piece was done for decorative purposes, because it was felt that many layers of wood were more interesting-looking than just one layer.

In addition to chip carving and layering, applied and inlaid decorations were another common feature used in Tramp Art. Since geometric patterns of circles, squares, and triangles were the easiest to carve, they were the most common type of applied and inlaid decoration. Hearts and stars were the most-used symbols for such decorations, and sometimes the entire object would be made into a heart shape.

Another type of tramp art that was sometimes produced, but was not quite as popular as the traditional layering and chip carving, is oftentimes referred to as the "crown of thorns." It was made in a layered manner and was also constructed with cigar-box wood. In this style, the piece of wood was notched together in an interlocking and overlapping fashion the way a log cabin is built. As the pieces were interlocked, they were also layered and built up like vertebrae to form a star effect.

Tramp art became a very popular art form because it allowed the tramp artisan to use the materials he had at hand to produce a great variety of things. Picture frames, gift and jewelry boxes, and full-size chests of drawers were created not only to fill his empty hours but so that they could be used as a gift for a friend, a barter for food or lodging, or an exchange for money. The tramp was likely to produce articles of a functional and practical nature, while the hobo whittled objects of art that were more whimsical and nonutilitarian.

How-To

*C*utting a series of angular notches that approximately equal the thickness of the wood. The exact spacing and style of notching should be developed by the individual. Some may prefer fewer notches with wider spacing and others may prefer to position the notches closer together; see Diagram 1 on the opposite page.

Diagram 1

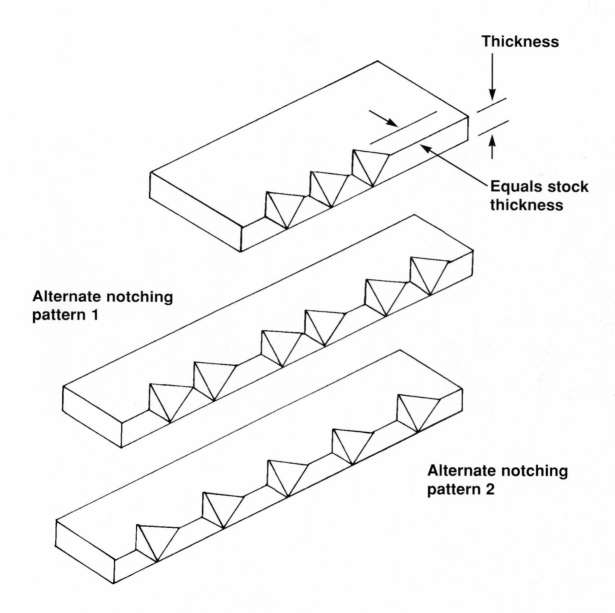

Thickness

Equals stock thickness

Alternate notching pattern 1

Alternate notching pattern 2

"Crown of thorns": This mysterious technique was practiced by only a very few tramp artists. It involved making pieces about ³⁄₁₆" square with pointed ends. They were also notched to fit together in a precise manner and an interlocking way. It is believed that the pieces were soaked in water prior to assembly to make the wood softer and pliable. The pieces would thus compress and slide into each other. The wood would spring back after assembly, holding the interlocking pieces secure and rigid.

Another interlocking work of tramp art. This item was used more as a puzzle novelty sort of thing than as an actual picture frame.

Old and authentic tramp art was made from old cigar box materials. These were a reddish color, usually fashioned of Spanish Mohagany, but many other odorless woods were also used.

Today, you can purchase thin woods, such as basswood, pine, redwood and other soft woods, that are already milled to thin, usable thicknesses and are easy to work with. Standard thicknesses also vary and are left to the choice of the artist or availability.

The beginning of a tramp
box: In this case, a real
cigar box provides the
basic form. All of the
pyramid layers are cut and
notched, ready to cover the
front surface.

A basic covered box (cigar size), with a double-pyramid design for its top. This box was made of dark wood and stained and varnished.

This photo shows how crudely some tramp art boxes were made. Notice the unusual effect of the picture frames built in around the sides and ends of the box.

An example of a small box with added decorative elements applied to the top and bottom. It is designed to form an unusual double-pedestal base. This box is made of pine with a natural unstained finish.

Frame

Shown is a simple wood frame, made of pine boards and cardboard patterns of the geometric design elements prepared to the desired size and shape for the very first layer of the notched pieces.

Each person created their own designs, often incorporating circles, squares, triangles, ovals, hearts, or a combination of geometric shapes. There were no hard and fast rules. Material thicknesses and spacing of notches varied with the individual. The size and placement of notches were not measured, but cut by "eye" and became remarkably uniform from layer to layer.

It is best to cover one layer on one surface completely, cutting each part to fit while at the same time checking the design layout before proceeding on to the next layer. Patterns made of cardboard help in checking the design layout as well as serving as actual patterns for cutting the wood pieces.

If trying to replicate a covered cigar box, the most popular size was 2½" x 6" x 8½". However, some boxes were up to 17" in length. The cigar boxes were made from ⅛" to 3⁄16" thick material. Very large frames and some other large boxes were made simply by butting smaller or shorter pieces end to end and staggering the joints within successive layers.

Glues were, as a rule, not used in Hobo or Tramp art projects because the granular animal glues available at the time required heating pots for use. Tramps and hobos did not have access to this type of equipment. Consequently, everything was nailed together with shoemaker's nails which were small tacks. Nails were often left exposed in the top layers. *Caution:* If you use glues, remember to be careful because the glue will seal the wood and it will not take stain or finishes uniformly. Areas where glue has squeezed out and spotted surfaces resulting from glue on your fingers will create a very splotchy and unattractive finish.

Most early Tramp art was brush-coated with several thick applications of a varnish stain. Some artists used oil stains. This picture frame project features a combination of stained pieces (inside and outside edges) and natural pieces. (Actually, it was coated with a 50-50 mixture of linseed oil and turpentine.)

Hobo art carvings were by and large left unfinished. The surfaces were seldom sanded. If a smooth surface was desired, knife marks were smoothed down with the edge of a broken piece of glass that served as a very effective scraping tool.

Section of frame stock and notched edge covering layers, Full size

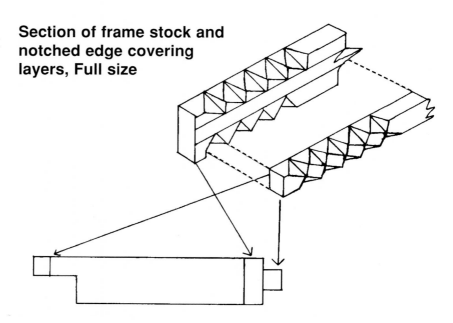

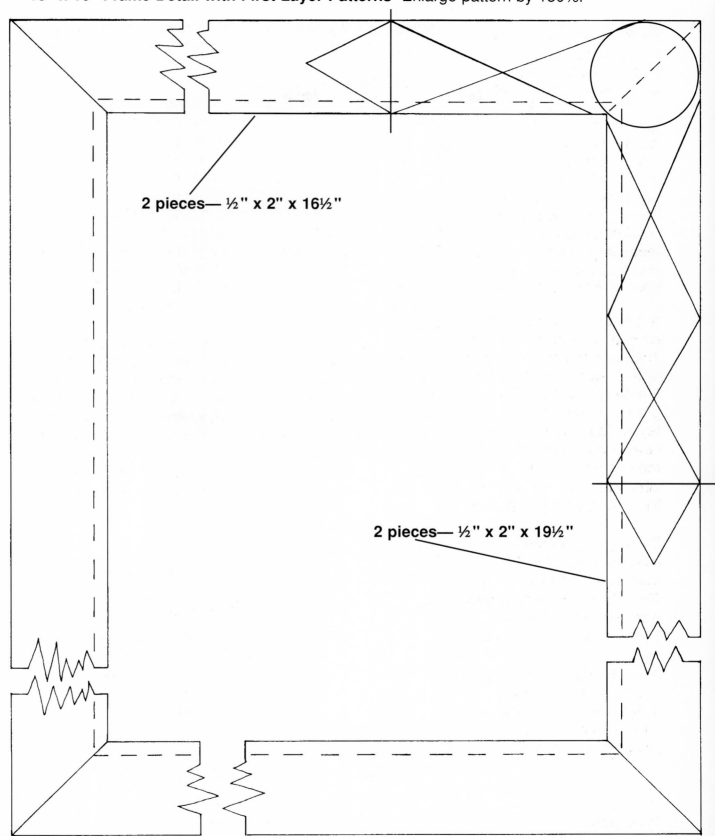

13" x 16" Frame Detail with First Layer Patterns Enlarge pattern by 150%.

2 pieces— ½" x 2" x 16½"

2 pieces— ½" x 2" x 19½"

Checking the layout and placement of the pattern designs on the frame surface.

*T*ransferring the patterns to
the surface of the wood.

*P*ositioning and tacking down the first layer. Originally, the artist used shoemaker's nails, which he obtained by bartering or "mooching."

*T*oday, use small brads and
just nail the pieces down.

Complete the first course
entirely before starting the
second course.

Starting the subsequent layers: Each successive layer should be reduced in size all around a distance that equals the approximate thickness of the material being used. *Note:* If you are using ¼"-thick stock, then cut each successive layer ¼" smaller all around. Thinner pieces and more layers make the project more interesting and obviously more valuable because of the time and effort required to complete the pyramidal shape.

"Finger-guaging" a line parallel to an edge: This technique is helpful and quickens the reduction of the size of the pattern which was previously used to mark out the piece of the previous layer.

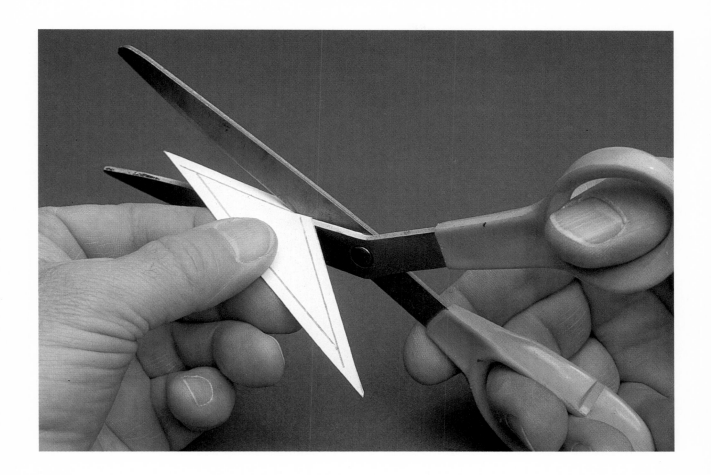

*C*utting down an existing
pattern to make a new one
for the following smaller
layer.

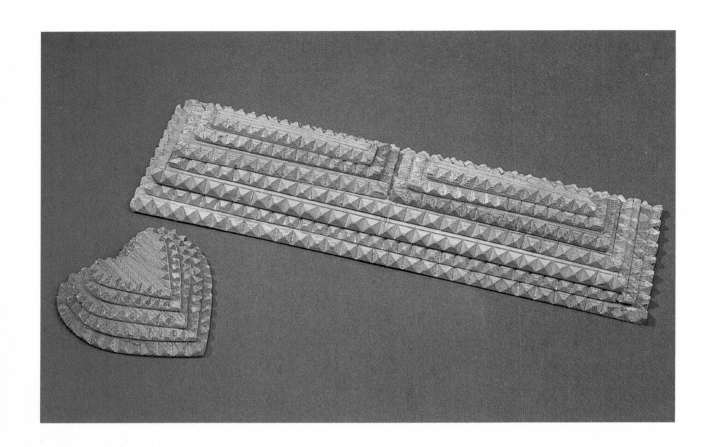

Some layering patterns that
can be used to cover
frames, boxes, or anything
else.

*T*he completed corner of
the frame project.

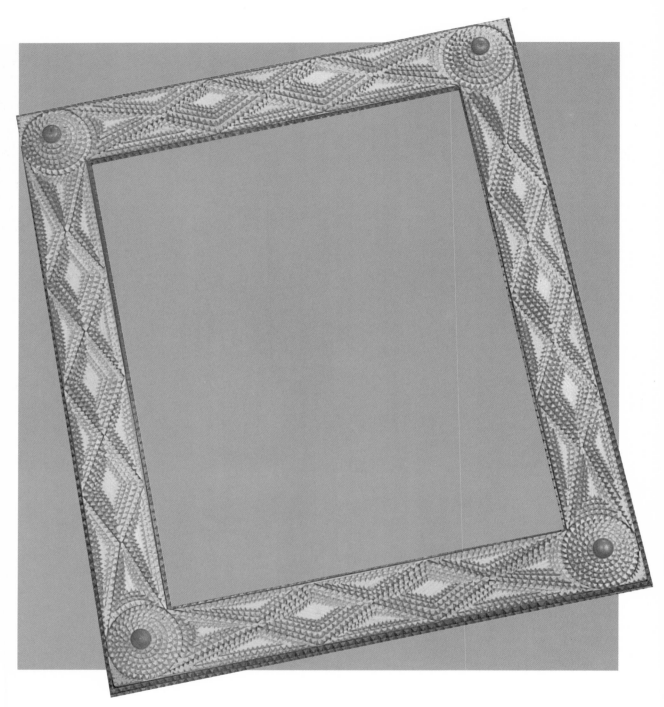

Completed frame.

*L*ayering can stop or be topped off with other decorative embellishments as desired. One popular decorative item was upholsterer's tacks made of brass.

Note how darker layers
were applied to the inside
and outside edges to cover
the pine substrate. Also,
note that the extreme outer
edge consists of just one layer.

Another frame showing
optional corner design.

Gallery

Tramp, tramp, tramp keep on trampin
Nothin doin here for you
If I catch you round again
You will wear the ball and chain
Keep on trampin that's the best thing
you can do.

— *Traditional hobo verse*

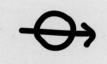

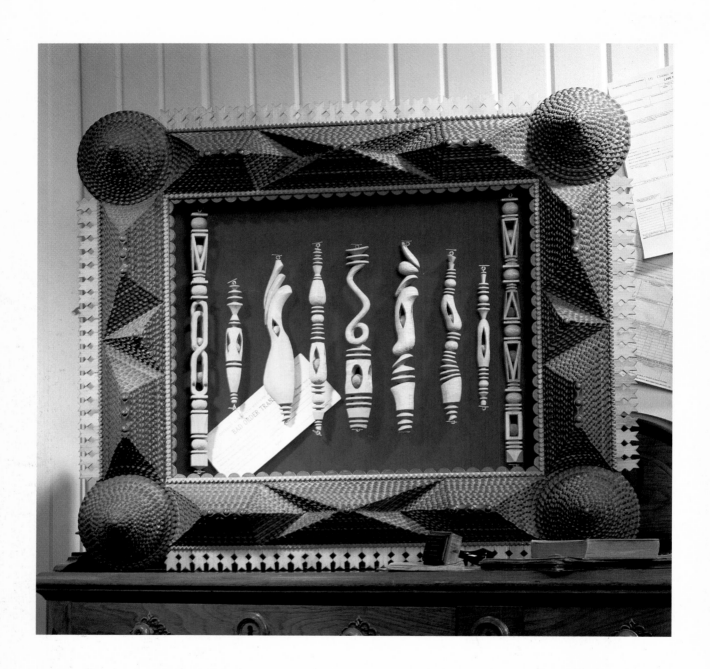

I've decked the tops of flying cars
That leaped across the night
The long and level coaches skimmed
Low, like a swallow's flight.

Close to the sleet-bit blinds I've clung
Rocking on and on;
All night I've crouched in empty cars
That rode into the dawn.

— Harry Kemp, hobo poet

Code to Hobo Signs

To complement the hobo art and tramp art projects and galleries, we have included several hobo signs. These symbols (and a few extras) would have been chalked on curbs or left in pencil on door facings, mailboxes, and gates. These markers were part of a code that served to guide a fellow wanderer toward good food and safe shelter and away from any danger or discomfort. It is recorded that there are thousands of hobo signs for thousands of occasions.

A good road to follow.

If you are sick, you'll find care here.

Here. This is the place.

A picture of a cat signals of a kind woman.

O.K. or all right.

You may camp here.

This is a good place for a handout.

This way.

(A top hat) A gentleman lives here.

A good place to catch a train.

Fresh water and a safe campsite.

No use going in this direction.

A mark of personal belongings.

A trolly stop.

Patrick Spielman

Patrick Spielman lives surrounded by a natural forest in the famous tourist area of Door County in northeast Wisconsin. A graduate of the University of Wisconsin-Stout, he taught high school and vocational woodworking in Wisconsin public schools for 27 years.

Patrick's love for wood and woodworking began between the ages of 8 and 10, when he transformed wooden fruit crates into toys. Encouragement from his parents, two older brothers, and a sister, who provided basic tools to keep the youngster occupied, enabled Patrick to become a very productive woodworker at an early age.

Today, he and his wife, Patricia, own Spielman's Wood Works and Spielman's Kid Works. Both are gift galleries that offer high-quality hand- and machine-crafted wood products produced locally and from around the world.

Patrick left the school classroom 10 years ago, but he continues to teach and share ideas and designs through his published works. He enjoys consulting and lending his knowledge of technical aspects of woodworking, as he has in this publication, to promote the talent and activities of other artisans. He has written over 50 woodworking books with some translated into Dutch and German.

One of Patrick's proudest accomplishments is his book, The Router Handbook, which has sold over 1.5 million copies worldwide. His updated version, The New Router Handbook, was selected the best how-to book of 1994 by the National Association of Home and Workshop writers. He is currently working on two new titles: The Art of the Router and The Art of the Lathe.

Metric Equivalency Chart

MM-Millimetres   CM-Centimetres

INCHES TO MILLIMETRES AND CENTIMETRES

INCHES	MM	CM	INCHES	CM	INCHES	CM
⅛	3	0.3	9	22.9	30	76.2
¼	6	0.6	10	25.4	31	78.7
½	13	1.3	12	30.5	33	83.8
⅝	16	1.6	13	33.0	34	86.4
¾	19	1.9	14	35.6	35	88.9
⅞	22	2.2	15	38.1	36	91.4
1	25	2.5	16	40.6	37	94.0
1¼	32	3.2	17	43.2	38	96.5
1½	38	3.8	18	45.7	39	99.1
1¾	44	4.4	19	48.3	40	101.6
2	51	5.1	20	50.8	41	104.1
2½	64	6.4	21	53.3	42	106.7
3	76	7.6	22	55.9	43	109.2
3½	89	8.9	23	58.4	44	111.8
4	102	10.2	24	61.0	45	114.3
4½	114	11.4	25	63.5	46	116.8
5	127	12.7	26	66.0	47	119.4
6	152	15.2	27	68.6	48	121.9
7	178	17.8	28	71.1	49	124.5
8	203	20.3	29	73.7	50	127.0

YARDS TO METRES

YARDS	METRES	YARDS	METRES	YARDS	METRES	YARDS	METRES	YARDS	METRES
⅛	0.11	2⅛	1.94	4⅛	3.77	6⅛	5.60	8⅛	7.43
¼	0.23	2¼	2.06	4¼	3.89	6¼	5.72	8¼	7.54
⅜	0.34	2⅜	2.17	4⅜	4.00	6⅜	5.83	8⅜	7.66
½	0.46	2½	2.29	4½	4.11	6½	5.94	8½	7.77
⅝	0.57	2⅝	2.40	4⅝	4.23	6⅝	6.06	8⅝	7.89
¾	0.69	2¾	2.51	4¾	4.34	6¾	6.17	8¾	8.00
⅞	0.80	2⅞	2.63	4⅞	4.46	6⅞	6.29	8⅞	8.12
1	0.91	3	2.74	5	4.57	7	6.40	9	8.23
1⅛	1.03	3⅛	2.86	5⅛	4.69	7⅛	6.52	9⅛	8.34
1¼	1.14	3¼	2.97	5¼	4.80	7¼	6.63	9¼	8.46
1⅜	1.26	3⅜	3.09	5⅜	4.91	7⅜	6.74	9⅜	8.57
1½	1.37	3½	3.20	5½	5.03	7½	6.86	9½	8.69
1⅝	1.49	3⅝	3.31	5⅝	5.14	7⅝	6.97	9⅝	8.80
1¾	1.60	3¾	3.43	5¾	5.26	7¾	7.09	9¾	8.92
1⅞	1.71	3⅞	3.54	5⅞	5.37	7⅞	7.20	9⅞	9.03
2	1.83	4	3.66	6	5.49	8	7.32	10	9.14

Index